50 Last-Minute Dinner Fixes Recipes for Home

By: Kelly Johnson

Table of Contents

- Garlic Butter Shrimp Pasta
- One-Pan Lemon Chicken and Asparagus
- Quick Beef Stir-Fry
- Caprese Stuffed Chicken
- Veggie Fried Rice
- Tuna Salad Wraps
- Skillet Chicken Fajitas
- Instant Pot Chili
- 15-Minute Shrimp Tacos
- Spinach and Feta Omelette
- Sausage and Peppers Sheet Pan Dinner
- Zucchini Noodles with Pesto
- Tomato Basil Soup with Grilled Cheese
- Greek Yogurt Chicken Salad
- Black Bean Quesadillas
- 10-Minute Teriyaki Salmon
- Spaghetti Aglio e Olio
- Egg Fried Rice
- Chickpea Salad
- Beef and Broccoli
- Pesto Pasta with Cherry Tomatoes
- Thai Peanut Chicken Lettuce Wraps
- Quinoa and Black Bean Bowl
- Lemon Garlic Tilapia
- Loaded Nachos
- Shrimp Scampi
- Creamy Tomato Pasta
- Spinach and Ricotta Stuffed Shells
- Instant Ramen with Vegetables
- Chicken Caesar Wraps
- Vegetable Stir-Fry
- Balsamic Glazed Chicken
- Tofu Pad Thai
- Breakfast Burritos
- Minestrone Soup

- Baked Sweet Potatoes with Black Beans
- Beef Tacos
- Greek Pasta Salad
- Spicy Chickpea Tacos
- Sesame Chicken
- Creamy Mushroom Risotto
- Roasted Vegetable and Hummus Wraps
- Garlic Parmesan Chicken Wings
- Pasta Primavera
- Sloppy Joes
- BBQ Chicken Pizza
- Stuffed Peppers
- Lobster Roll Sliders
- Curry Lentil Soup
- Vegetable Quesadillas

Garlic Butter Shrimp Pasta

Ingredients:

- 8 oz spaghetti
- 1 lb shrimp, peeled and deveined
- 4 tbsp butter
- 4 cloves garlic, minced
- 1/2 tsp red pepper flakes (optional)
- Salt and pepper, to taste
- 2 tbsp lemon juice
- Fresh parsley, chopped (for garnish)

Instructions:

1. Cook spaghetti according to package instructions. Drain and set aside.
2. In a large skillet, melt butter over medium heat. Add garlic and red pepper flakes; sauté for 1-2 minutes until fragrant.
3. Add shrimp, season with salt and pepper, and cook until pink, about 3-4 minutes.
4. Stir in lemon juice and cooked pasta, tossing to combine.
5. Garnish with parsley and serve immediately.

Enjoy your delicious Garlic Butter Shrimp Pasta!

One-Pan Lemon Chicken and Asparagus

Ingredients:

- 4 chicken breasts
- 1 lb asparagus, trimmed
- 3 tbsp olive oil
- 2 lemons (juiced and zested)
- 4 cloves garlic, minced
- Salt and pepper, to taste

Instructions:

1. Preheat oven to 400°F (200°C).
2. In a bowl, mix olive oil, lemon juice, zest, garlic, salt, and pepper.
3. Place chicken and asparagus on a baking sheet; pour the mixture over them.
4. Bake for 25-30 minutes until chicken is cooked through. Serve hot.

Quick Beef Stir-Fry

Ingredients:

- 1 lb beef sirloin, sliced thinly
- 2 cups mixed bell peppers, sliced
- 3 cloves garlic, minced
- 2 tbsp soy sauce
- 2 tbsp vegetable oil
- Cooked rice, for serving

Instructions:

1. Heat oil in a pan over high heat. Add beef and cook for 2-3 minutes until browned.
2. Add garlic and bell peppers; stir-fry for another 3-4 minutes.
3. Pour in soy sauce, stir to combine, and serve over rice.

Caprese Stuffed Chicken

Ingredients:

- 4 chicken breasts
- 1 cup mozzarella cheese, shredded
- 2 tomatoes, diced
- Fresh basil leaves
- 2 tbsp balsamic glaze
- Salt and pepper, to taste

Instructions:

1. Preheat oven to 375°F (190°C). Slice each chicken breast to create a pocket.
2. Stuff each pocket with mozzarella, tomatoes, and basil. Season with salt and pepper.
3. Place in a baking dish, drizzle with balsamic glaze, and bake for 25-30 minutes until cooked through.

Enjoy your cooking!

Veggie Fried Rice

Ingredients:

- 3 cups cooked rice
- 2 cups mixed vegetables (carrots, peas, bell peppers)
- 2 eggs, beaten
- 3 tbsp soy sauce
- 2 tbsp sesame oil
- Green onions, for garnish

Instructions:

1. Heat sesame oil in a pan. Add mixed vegetables and stir-fry for 3-4 minutes.
2. Push veggies to the side, pour in eggs, and scramble.
3. Add cooked rice and soy sauce; stir to combine and heat through. Garnish with green onions.

Tuna Salad Wraps

Ingredients:

- 1 can tuna, drained
- 2 tbsp mayonnaise
- 1 tbsp Dijon mustard
- Lettuce leaves
- Tomato, sliced
- Salt and pepper, to taste

Instructions:

1. In a bowl, mix tuna, mayonnaise, mustard, salt, and pepper.
2. Spoon the mixture onto lettuce leaves, top with tomato, and wrap.

Skillet Chicken Fajitas

Ingredients:

- 1 lb chicken breast, sliced
- 1 bell pepper, sliced
- 1 onion, sliced
- 2 tbsp fajita seasoning
- Tortillas, for serving

Instructions:

1. In a skillet, cook chicken until browned.
2. Add bell pepper, onion, and fajita seasoning; sauté until veggies are tender.
3. Serve in tortillas.

Instant Pot Chili

Ingredients:

- 1 lb ground beef
- 1 can kidney beans, drained
- 1 can diced tomatoes
- 1 onion, diced
- 2 tbsp chili powder
- Salt and pepper, to taste

Instructions:

1. Sauté onion and ground beef in the Instant Pot until browned.
2. Add beans, tomatoes, chili powder, salt, and pepper.
3. Cook on high pressure for 20 minutes, then release pressure.

15-Minute Shrimp Tacos

Ingredients:

- 1 lb shrimp, peeled and deveined
- 1 tbsp taco seasoning
- Corn tortillas
- Cabbage, shredded
- Lime wedges

Instructions:

1. Sauté shrimp with taco seasoning for 3-4 minutes until cooked.
2. Serve in tortillas with cabbage and lime wedges.

Spinach and Feta Omelette

Ingredients:

- 3 eggs
- 1 cup spinach, chopped
- 1/2 cup feta cheese
- Salt and pepper, to taste

Instructions:

1. Whisk eggs with salt and pepper.
2. Pour into a heated skillet, add spinach and feta, and cook until set.

Sausage and Peppers Sheet Pan Dinner

Ingredients:

- 1 lb sausage, sliced
- 2 bell peppers, sliced
- 1 onion, sliced
- 2 tbsp olive oil
- Salt and pepper, to taste

Instructions:

1. Preheat oven to 400°F (200°C).
2. Toss sausage and veggies with olive oil, salt, and pepper.
3. Spread on a sheet pan and roast for 25-30 minutes.

Zucchini Noodles with Pesto

Ingredients:

- 4 zucchini, spiralized
- 1/2 cup pesto
- Cherry tomatoes, halved
- Parmesan cheese, for serving

Instructions:

1. Sauté zucchini noodles in a pan for 2-3 minutes.
2. Toss with pesto and cherry tomatoes, then serve with Parmesan.

Enjoy your cooking!

Tomato Basil Soup with Grilled Cheese

Ingredients:

- 1 can crushed tomatoes
- 1 cup vegetable broth
- 1 onion, chopped
- 2 cloves garlic, minced
- Fresh basil, chopped
- Salt and pepper, to taste
- Bread and cheese for sandwiches

Instructions:

1. Sauté onion and garlic until soft. Add crushed tomatoes and broth; simmer for 15 minutes.
2. Blend until smooth, stir in basil, and season.
3. For grilled cheese, butter bread, add cheese, and grill until golden. Serve together.

Greek Yogurt Chicken Salad

Ingredients:

- 2 cups cooked chicken, shredded
- 1/2 cup Greek yogurt
- 1/4 cup celery, chopped
- 1/4 cup grapes, halved
- Salt and pepper, to taste

Instructions:

1. In a bowl, combine chicken, Greek yogurt, celery, grapes, salt, and pepper.
2. Mix well and serve on lettuce or bread.

Black Bean Quesadillas

Ingredients:

- 1 can black beans, drained
- 1 cup cheese, shredded
- Tortillas
- Salsa, for serving

Instructions:

1. Spread black beans and cheese on one half of a tortilla; fold.
2. Cook in a skillet until golden, flipping once. Serve with salsa.

10-Minute Teriyaki Salmon

Ingredients:

- 2 salmon fillets
- 1/4 cup teriyaki sauce
- Green onions, for garnish

Instructions:

1. Heat a skillet over medium-high heat. Add salmon skin-side down.
2. Cook for 4-5 minutes, then flip and add teriyaki sauce. Cook for another 2-3 minutes. Garnish with green onions.

Spaghetti Aglio e Olio

Ingredients:

- 8 oz spaghetti
- 4 cloves garlic, sliced
- 1/2 tsp red pepper flakes
- 1/4 cup olive oil
- Fresh parsley, chopped

Instructions:

1. Cook spaghetti according to package instructions.
2. In a skillet, heat olive oil and sauté garlic and red pepper flakes.
3. Toss cooked spaghetti in the skillet and garnish with parsley.

Egg Fried Rice

Ingredients:

- 3 cups cooked rice
- 2 eggs, beaten
- 1 cup mixed vegetables
- 2 tbsp soy sauce
- Green onions, for garnish

Instructions:

1. Heat oil in a pan. Scramble the eggs and set aside.
2. Sauté mixed vegetables, add rice and soy sauce, then stir in eggs. Garnish with green onions.

Chickpea Salad

Ingredients:

- 1 can chickpeas, drained
- 1 cucumber, diced
- 1 bell pepper, diced
- 1/4 cup red onion, diced
- Olive oil and lemon juice, for dressing

Instructions:

1. In a bowl, combine chickpeas, cucumber, bell pepper, and onion.
2. Drizzle with olive oil and lemon juice, then toss to combine.

Beef and Broccoli

Ingredients:

- 1 lb beef, sliced thin
- 2 cups broccoli florets
- 1/4 cup soy sauce
- 2 cloves garlic, minced
- 2 tbsp vegetable oil

Instructions:

1. Heat oil in a pan, add beef, and cook until browned.
2. Add garlic and broccoli, stir-fry for 3-4 minutes, then add soy sauce. Serve hot.

Enjoy your cooking!

Pesto Pasta with Cherry Tomatoes

Ingredients:

- 8 oz pasta
- 1 cup pesto
- 1 cup cherry tomatoes, halved
- Parmesan cheese, for serving

Instructions:

1. Cook pasta according to package instructions; drain.
2. Toss with pesto and cherry tomatoes.
3. Serve topped with Parmesan cheese.

Thai Peanut Chicken Lettuce Wraps

Ingredients:

- 2 cups cooked chicken, shredded
- 1/2 cup peanut sauce
- Lettuce leaves
- Carrots, shredded
- Chopped peanuts, for garnish

Instructions:

1. Mix chicken with peanut sauce.
2. Spoon mixture onto lettuce leaves, top with carrots and peanuts.

Quinoa and Black Bean Bowl

Ingredients:

- 1 cup quinoa, cooked
- 1 can black beans, drained
- 1 cup corn
- 1 avocado, diced
- Lime juice, for dressing

Instructions:

1. In a bowl, combine quinoa, black beans, corn, and avocado.
2. Drizzle with lime juice and toss to combine.

Lemon Garlic Tilapia

Ingredients:

- 4 tilapia fillets
- 2 tbsp olive oil
- 2 cloves garlic, minced
- Juice of 1 lemon
- Salt and pepper, to taste

Instructions:

1. Preheat oven to 400°F (200°C).
2. Place tilapia on a baking sheet; drizzle with olive oil, garlic, lemon juice, salt, and pepper.
3. Bake for 15-20 minutes until cooked through.

Loaded Nachos

Ingredients:

- Tortilla chips
- 1 cup cheese, shredded
- 1 can black beans, drained
- Jalapeños, sliced
- Sour cream, for serving

Instructions:

1. Preheat oven to 350°F (175°C).
2. Layer chips, cheese, black beans, and jalapeños on a baking sheet.
3. Bake for 10 minutes until cheese melts; serve with sour cream.

Shrimp Scampi

Ingredients:

- 1 lb shrimp, peeled and deveined
- 4 cloves garlic, minced
- 1/2 cup white wine
- 1/4 cup butter
- Cooked pasta, for serving

Instructions:

1. In a skillet, melt butter; add garlic and sauté for 1 minute.
2. Add shrimp and cook until pink. Pour in white wine and simmer for 2-3 minutes.
3. Serve over cooked pasta.

Creamy Tomato Pasta

Ingredients:

- 8 oz pasta
- 1 can crushed tomatoes
- 1/2 cup heavy cream
- 2 cloves garlic, minced
- Basil, for garnish

Instructions:

1. Cook pasta according to package instructions; drain.
2. In a skillet, combine crushed tomatoes, cream, and garlic; simmer for 5 minutes.
3. Toss with pasta and garnish with basil.

Spinach and Ricotta Stuffed Shells

Ingredients:

- 12 jumbo pasta shells
- 1 cup ricotta cheese
- 2 cups spinach, cooked
- 1 cup marinara sauce
- 1 cup mozzarella cheese, shredded

Instructions:

1. Preheat oven to 375°F (190°C).
2. Cook shells according to package instructions; drain.
3. Mix ricotta and spinach, stuff into shells, and place in a baking dish.
4. Top with marinara and mozzarella; bake for 25-30 minutes.

Enjoy your cooking!

Instant Ramen with Vegetables

Ingredients:

- 2 packs instant ramen
- 2 cups mixed vegetables (fresh or frozen)
- 2 green onions, chopped
- Soy sauce, to taste

Instructions:

1. Cook ramen according to package instructions; add mixed vegetables in the last few minutes.
2. Drain excess water, add soy sauce, and garnish with green onions.

Chicken Caesar Wraps

Ingredients:

- 2 cups cooked chicken, shredded
- 1 cup romaine lettuce, chopped
- 1/2 cup Caesar dressing
- Tortillas
- Parmesan cheese, for garnish

Instructions:

1. In a bowl, mix chicken, lettuce, and Caesar dressing.
2. Spoon mixture onto tortillas, sprinkle with Parmesan, and wrap.

Vegetable Stir-Fry

Ingredients:

- 3 cups mixed vegetables (broccoli, bell peppers, carrots)
- 2 tbsp soy sauce
- 1 tbsp vegetable oil
- Cooked rice, for serving

Instructions:

1. Heat oil in a pan; add vegetables and stir-fry for 5-7 minutes.
2. Add soy sauce and cook for another minute. Serve over rice.

Balsamic Glazed Chicken

Ingredients:

- 4 chicken breasts
- 1/2 cup balsamic vinegar
- 2 tbsp honey
- Salt and pepper, to taste

Instructions:

1. Preheat oven to 400°F (200°C).
2. Mix balsamic vinegar, honey, salt, and pepper; pour over chicken in a baking dish.
3. Bake for 25-30 minutes until cooked through.

Tofu Pad Thai

Ingredients:

- 8 oz rice noodles
- 1 block firm tofu, cubed
- 2 cups mixed vegetables
- 1/4 cup pad Thai sauce
- Lime wedges, for serving

Instructions:

1. Cook noodles according to package instructions; drain.
2. In a skillet, sauté tofu until golden; add vegetables and cook for 3-4 minutes.
3. Add noodles and pad Thai sauce, toss to combine, and serve with lime wedges.

Breakfast Burritos

Ingredients:

- 4 eggs, scrambled
- 1 cup cooked sausage or bacon
- 1/2 cup cheese, shredded
- Tortillas
- Salsa, for serving

Instructions:

1. Mix scrambled eggs with sausage and cheese.
2. Spoon the mixture onto tortillas, wrap, and serve with salsa.

Minestrone Soup

Ingredients:

- 1 can diced tomatoes
- 1 can kidney beans, drained
- 2 cups mixed vegetables
- 4 cups vegetable broth
- Italian seasoning, to taste

Instructions:

1. In a pot, combine all ingredients and bring to a boil.
2. Simmer for 20-30 minutes until veggies are tender.

Baked Sweet Potatoes with Black Beans

Ingredients:

- 2 sweet potatoes
- 1 can black beans, drained
- 1 avocado, diced
- Lime juice, for drizzling

Instructions:

1. Preheat oven to 400°F (200°C). Prick sweet potatoes and bake for 45-60 minutes until tender.
2. Slice open, fill with black beans and avocado, and drizzle with lime juice.

Enjoy your cooking!

Beef Tacos

Ingredients:

- 1 lb ground beef
- 1 taco seasoning packet
- Tortillas
- Toppings: lettuce, cheese, salsa, avocado

Instructions:

1. Cook ground beef in a skillet until browned; add taco seasoning and water as directed on the packet.
2. Serve in tortillas with your choice of toppings.

Greek Pasta Salad

Ingredients:

- 8 oz pasta, cooked and cooled
- 1 cup cherry tomatoes, halved
- 1 cucumber, diced
- 1/2 cup feta cheese, crumbled
- 1/4 cup olives, sliced
- Olive oil and lemon juice, for dressing

Instructions:

1. In a large bowl, combine pasta, tomatoes, cucumber, feta, and olives.
2. Drizzle with olive oil and lemon juice; toss to combine.

Spicy Chickpea Tacos

Ingredients:

- 1 can chickpeas, drained
- 2 tbsp olive oil
- 1 tsp chili powder
- Tortillas
- Toppings: avocado, cilantro, lime

Instructions:

1. In a skillet, heat olive oil; add chickpeas and chili powder, cooking until heated through.
2. Serve in tortillas with avocado, cilantro, and lime.

Sesame Chicken

Ingredients:

- 1 lb chicken breast, cubed
- 1/4 cup soy sauce
- 2 tbsp sesame oil
- 1 tbsp honey
- Sesame seeds, for garnish

Instructions:

1. In a skillet, heat sesame oil; add chicken and cook until browned.
2. Stir in soy sauce and honey, cooking for another 2-3 minutes. Garnish with sesame seeds.

Creamy Mushroom Risotto

Ingredients:

- 1 cup Arborio rice
- 4 cups vegetable broth
- 1 cup mushrooms, sliced
- 1 onion, diced
- 1/2 cup Parmesan cheese

Instructions:

1. In a pot, sauté onion and mushrooms until soft.
2. Add Arborio rice and gradually stir in broth until creamy. Mix in Parmesan before serving.

Roasted Vegetable and Hummus Wraps

Ingredients:

- 2 cups mixed vegetables (zucchini, bell peppers, carrots)
- 1 cup hummus
- Tortillas

Instructions:

1. Preheat oven to 400°F (200°C); roast vegetables for 20-25 minutes.
2. Spread hummus on tortillas, add roasted veggies, and wrap.

Garlic Parmesan Chicken Wings

Ingredients:

- 2 lbs chicken wings
- 4 cloves garlic, minced
- 1/4 cup Parmesan cheese, grated
- 2 tbsp butter, melted

Instructions:

1. Preheat oven to 425°F (220°C). Toss wings with garlic and melted butter.
2. Bake for 30-35 minutes until crispy; sprinkle with Parmesan before serving.

Pasta Primavera

Ingredients:

- 8 oz pasta
- 2 cups mixed vegetables (bell peppers, broccoli, carrots)
- 2 tbsp olive oil
- Parmesan cheese, for serving

Instructions:

1. Cook pasta according to package instructions; drain.
2. Sauté vegetables in olive oil until tender, then toss with pasta and serve with Parmesan.

Enjoy your cooking!

Sloppy Joes

Ingredients:

- 1 lb ground beef
- 1/2 onion, chopped
- 1/2 cup ketchup
- 2 tbsp Worcestershire sauce
- 1 tbsp brown sugar
- Salt and pepper, to taste
- Hamburger buns

Instructions:

1. In a skillet, cook ground beef and onion until beef is browned.
2. Stir in ketchup, Worcestershire sauce, brown sugar, salt, and pepper; simmer for 5 minutes.
3. Serve on hamburger buns.

BBQ Chicken Pizza

Ingredients:

- 1 pizza crust
- 1 cup cooked chicken, shredded
- 1/2 cup BBQ sauce
- 1 cup cheese, shredded (mozzarella or cheddar)
- Red onion, thinly sliced

Instructions:

1. Preheat oven according to pizza crust instructions.
2. Mix chicken with BBQ sauce and spread over the crust.
3. Top with cheese and red onion slices; bake until cheese is melted.

Stuffed Peppers

Ingredients:

- 4 bell peppers, halved and seeded
- 1 lb ground beef or turkey
- 1 cup cooked rice
- 1 can diced tomatoes
- 1 tsp Italian seasoning
- Cheese, for topping

Instructions:

1. Preheat oven to 375°F (190°C).
2. In a skillet, cook meat until browned; stir in rice, tomatoes, and seasoning.
3. Fill pepper halves with mixture, top with cheese, and bake for 30-35 minutes.

Lobster Roll Sliders

Ingredients:

- 1 lb cooked lobster meat, chopped
- 1/4 cup mayonnaise
- 1 tbsp lemon juice
- 1/4 cup celery, diced
- Slider rolls

Instructions:

1. In a bowl, mix lobster meat, mayonnaise, lemon juice, and celery.
2. Serve the mixture in slider rolls.

Curry Lentil Soup

Ingredients:

- 1 cup lentils, rinsed
- 1 onion, chopped
- 2 cloves garlic, minced
- 2 carrots, diced
- 4 cups vegetable broth
- 1 tbsp curry powder
- Salt and pepper, to taste

Instructions:

1. In a pot, sauté onion and garlic until soft.
2. Add carrots, lentils, broth, curry powder, salt, and pepper; bring to a boil.
3. Simmer for 25-30 minutes until lentils are tender.

Vegetable Quesadillas

Ingredients:

- 2 cups mixed vegetables (bell peppers, zucchini, spinach)
- 1 cup cheese, shredded
- Tortillas
- Salsa, for serving

Instructions:

1. Sauté mixed vegetables until tender.
2. Place cheese and veggies between tortillas; cook in a skillet until golden, flipping once.
3. Cut into wedges and serve with salsa.

Enjoy your cooking!